WORK HARD
&
BE NICE
TO PEOPLE

START WITH YES

This book began life as a paperback version of my previous book, MAKE IT NOW! and developed into a completely refreshed edition. Applying lessons from my first book, and editing and condensing existing content, my Publisher and I crafted this exciting new distillation. So this isn't exactly the same book as before but shares some ideas and approaches alongside new insights and developments.

This is the introduction. It's here to start our conversation. I am saying "hello" to you. Thank you for picking up this book and getting this far. I can tell you're already interested in what I've got to say. Or maybe you were given this book by somebody else and you've only just got round to actually reading it. I'm sorry, but this is going to be quite a one-sided conversation. I've already decided what I'm going to say, it's written down in this book. You'll just have to read it and make your own mind up. Why are you here? What do you want? What are you hoping to learn from this book? I haven't got all the answers to your questions. I'm suspicious of people who seem to have all the answers.

Taking advice from somebody who has never met you feels like taking a leap into the unknown. You don't need to read this book – you already know what's best for you. Maybe you just need to know that what you suspect is correct, an affirmation that your hunch is valid. I would like you to read this book; there might be some ideas that connect with you. Then my job will have been done succesfully.

NEW IDEAS ARE NEW

The familiar is a comfortable place to be. There are no surprises, we know what's going to happen next, there is nothing that's going to challenge us or question our choices.

The un-familiar can be an uncomfortable place to be. It's full of surprises and we don't know what's going to happen next. New ideas will challenge us and question our choices.

LEARN TO LOOK

LEARN TO SEE

Is everything really what it appears to be?

How can we be sure that what we are experiencing is what we think it is?

Never take anything at face value, look behind the surface. What is really going on?

It's good not to know things sometimes.
You don't start with all the answers.
If you know what the outcome is going
to be before you start, then why are you
doing it? Isn't it more fun to explore new
ideas and ways of working rather than
treading the same old path? Trust your
first response to something new.
If you like it, then you like it.
If you don't like it, then you don't like it.

I LIKE IT. WHAT IS IT?
WHAT IS IT? I LIKE IT.
I LIKE IT. WHAT IS IT?
WHAT IS IT? I LIKE IT.
I LIKE IT. WHAT IS IT?
WHAT IS IT? I LIKE IT.
I LIKE IT. WHAT IS IT?
WHAT IS IT? I LIKE IT.
I LIKE IT. WHAT IS IT?

QUESTION ACCEPTED WISDOM

This is how new ideas happen.
By questioning what went before we can make something new.

Everything changes
every day.

What was valid yesterday
is useless today.

Creativity grows and
adapts as a response
to what is happening
around it.

EXPERIMENT

Don't be afraid to experiment and try something new. Your first attempt will be a disaster (unless you are very lucky). Don't be put off. Try it again, keep trying and put your learning into practice. Don't compare yourself to other people who might be more experienced than you. Of course, you need to look up to work you admire, but don't be put off trying new things just because you think you won't be any good.

Ignore the doubting voice in your head and dive in with energy and enthusiasm.

DON'T BE AFRAID TO MAKE MISTAKES

Getting things wrong is key to the creative process. If you're afraid of getting things wrong you'll hold yourself back. Test your ideas to destruction. Don't be afraid of pulling everything apart and taking a U-turn. Allow yourself to think creatively. Don't put barriers up between what you think you can do and what you can actually do. You'll be surprised what you are capable of.

WHERE ARE WE?

**Find the
extraordinary
in the ordinary.**

Being in a new environment
forces you to question
yourself about everything.

Changing your daily routine
makes you look at the world
through fresh eyes.

You can discover more in the
first day somewhere new than
in a week at home.

Document everything, take
photographs, collect things
and keep mementoes.

Seeing the world helps you to
put you and your work in
context.

Originality comes out of combining influences and experiences in a new and interesting way.

WHO MADE THE RULES

Why do we obey rules that don't apply to us?

Why are we constrained by rules that other people invented? I'm not talking about rules like, *don't walk on railway lines*. I'm thinking about boring rules that prevent you from trying new ideas and developing new ways of working.

You can't do that / You can do this – Please, don't tell me what I can and can't do, what I can and can't think.

Conformity is the opposite of creativity – as soon as you start doing as you are told and follow the rules, you stop being truly creative.

Don't accept that things are always done in a certain way. Find out why things are done the way they are, then find out if there are better ways of doing them.

There's a lot of pressure to conform, I like it when people don't. I like oddballs (I may even be one myself). I admire individuals who do their own thing and have a unique view of the world. The interesting stuff is always on the fringes of society, never the mainstream. Unconventional people are ingenious and inventive; it's inspiring to see the world through their eyes.

It takes mavericks to show there is another way for everybody else; they are the pathfinders for new ways of living.

DON'T BE
NORMAL
DON'T BE
ORDINARY

NOBODY IS

We all feel we are unique and have our own particular way of looking at the world.

**Your individuality is
what makes you, you.**

**You need to be
yourself to be
happy.**

YOU KNOW MORE

Break bad habits that derail your creative flow. Pull apart your creative process and identify the parts that don't work. Fix the broken connections that stop you doing what you want to do. Stop giving yourself excuses to avoid doing things that you know you should do. If it seems too much to tackle everything in one go, break it into manageable pieces that you can solve quickly. The answer is always in the question. If it's the right question!

THAN YOU THINK

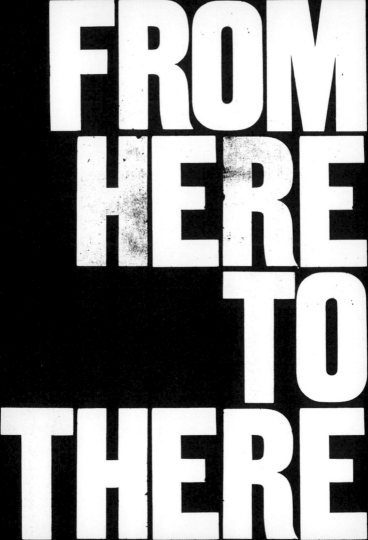

FROM
HERE
TO
THERE

FROM
THEN
TO
NOW

Picture where you want to be, then work out how to get there.

Work on as many ideas as you can.
Even the weak ones will act as a
springboard into a new way of thinking.
Don't edit yourself, let the ideas flow out.
Use ideas as a pathway, let them act as
signal markers on your path to a great idea.

EVERY IDEA IS A USEFUL IDEA

SAY WHAT YOU MEAN

Be brave, speak your mind and don't be afraid to talk about your ideas.

MEAN WHAT YOU SAY

Get over your shyness and build your confidence.

You'll be admired for saying what you think, even if it goes against accepted wisdom. Have strength in your convictions. Say what you need to say.

Break your routine. If you're feeling stuck it's time to change everything. Change your surroundings, take in some new experiences. It's better to spend a day gathering new information than it is to feel stagnant and unproductive. Get outside and don't feel bad about not "working".

GO FOR A WALK
DO THE WASHING-UP
SEE AN EXHIBITION
LISTEN TO MUSIC
GO FOR A BIKE RIDE
MAKE A CUP OF TEA
WATCH A FILM
READ A BOOK
GO SWIMMING
HAVE A CONVERSATION
GO FOR A DAY TRIP

PERSISTENCE IS FRUITFUL

Never give up — you should be working to hone your approach and developing your voice at every stage of your career. Persevere and carry on knocking on doors and seeking out opportunities. It takes time to build your confidence. Surrounding yourself with people you trust and who you can bounce ideas off is vital for that process.

TURN EVERYTHING UPSIDE DOWN

Look at things from a different angle. A new viewpoint will provide new insights that can be turned into new ideas.

THIS IS WHO I AM

THIS IS

Trust your own instinct.
You know yourself
better than anyone.
Be proud of who you are
and defend your ideas.

WHERE
I AM

ASK YOURSELF

What do I have to say?
How do I fit into the world?
How do I want to change the
world around me?
What is it about me that is
different from everybody else?
How important is it to me that
I make work that I'm proud of?

KEEP ASKING YOURSELF

Have I been effective in
communicating my opinions
through my work?
Do I want to fit in or do
I want to make my own way?
Have I been successful in
changing things for me and
the people around me?
Is it still important to me
to pursue my personal goals?
Over the past twelve months
have I made work that I'm
proud of?

```
Insert
insightful
text
here
```

Add
thought-
provoking
words
here

HOW WHEN WHO WHAT
WHEN WHO WHAT HOW
WHO WHAT HOW WHEN
WHAT HOW WHEN WHO
HOW WHEN WHO WHAT
WHEN WHO WHAT HOW
WHO WHAT HOW WHEN
WHAT HOW WHEN WHO
HOW WHEN WHO WHAT
WHEN WHO WHAT HOW
WHO WHAT HOW WHEN
WHAT HOW WHEN WHO

You do your best work when you're not trying to please other people, just doing your own thing and pleasing yourself.

NOTHING HAPPENS WHEN NOTHING HAPPENS

NOTHING HAPPENS IF NOTHING HAPPENS

WE
SAY
YES
YOU
SAY
YES
I
SAY
YES

Working in a group is a good way of finding out more about yourself. Are you a leader and an organiser or are you happy to take a back seat and be told what to do?

YES

"YES.
I MEAN
NO!"

THINK IT UP

Work fast and let the ideas flow out, don't stifle your creative process with overanalysis.

Try an idea out. If it works that's great, if it doesn't, think of another one.

TRY IT OUT

Ideas come quickest when you're being playful – let the ideas out and see where they go.

GO EVERYWHERE
DO EVERYTHING
GO EVERYWHERE
DO EVERYTHING
GO EVERYWHERE
DO EVERYTHING

DO EVERYTHING
GO EVERYWHERE
DO EVERYTHING
GO EVERYWHERE
DO EVERYTHING
GO EVERYWHERE

THINK TOGETHER

MAKE TOGETHER

Humans are social animals, we like to be together in groups.

Interesting ideas come out when working with like-minded friends.

MAKE IT NEW MAKE IT NOW

Every day something new comes
along to excite and stimulate.
It's part of leading a creative
and happy life, to look and
discover. Then to turn those
discoveries into something useful
that can help make life fun
and worthwhile.

ME &
YOU

YOU
&ME

I WANT WHAT YOU WANT

I've always sought out collaborations, it makes working life more social and enjoyable.

I like the back and forth of a collaborative project, sharing ideas and working out new ways of doing things.

YOU WANT WHAT I WANT

WORK HARD

BE NICE TO PEOPLE

How many times have you heard this one? It's still true, it works.

I start work in my studio next door to my house at around 8:30 in the morning. I have various diversions and little rituals that I go through – choosing music, reading the news, tidying up and looking out of the window at the trees outside. These things might look like procrastination to the untrained eye, but this stuff is incredibly valuable. It gets me into the right frame of mind to work, it's like warming up before going for a run (I imagine).

I'm a big believer in working when it feels right and not forcing it too much. I think we only put things off that we are secretly dreading or having difficulty working out how to do. The best thing to do is just get on with it and stop diverting attention away from the job in hand. Once you get into it and start making, it will feel less of a chore and you can start to enjoy it.

THE IDEA IS THE WORK

Find the idea in your work. It's already there, you just have to seek it out and amplify the message.

THE
IDEA
MAKES
THE
WORK

ANSWER YOUR OWN QUESTION

QUESTION YOUR OWN ANSWER

YOUR RULES ARE NOT MY RULES

Rip up the rule book
Where do rules come from?
Ignore stupid rules
Make your own rules
Your rules are not my rules!

YES
OK!

OK!
YES

BORING BORING BORING BORING BORING BORING BORING
BORING BORING BORING BORING BORING BORING BORING
BORING BORING BORING BORING BORING BORING BORING
BORING BORING BORING BORING BORING BORING BORING
BORING BORING BORING BORING BORING BORING BORING
BORING BORING BORING BORING BORING BORING BORING
BORING BORING BORING BORING BORING BORING BORING
BORING BORING BORING BORING BORING BORING BORING
BORING BORING BORING BORING BORING BORING BORING
BORING BORING BORING BORING BORING BORING BORING
BORING BORING BORING BORING BORING BORING BORING
BORING BORING BORING BORING BORING BORING BORING
BORING BORING BORING BORING BORING BORING BORING
BORING BORING BORING BORING BORING BORING BORING
BORING BORING BORING BORING BORING BORING BORING
BORING BORING BORING BORING BORING BORING BORING
BORING BORING BORING BORING BORING BORING BORING
BORING BORING BORING BORING BORING BORING BORING
BORING BORING BORING BORING BORING BORING BORING
BORING BORING BORING BORING BORING BORING BORING
BORING BORING BORING BORING BORING BORING BORING
BORING BORING BORING BORING BORING BORING BORING
BORING BORING BORING BORING BORING BORING BORING
BORING BORING BORING BORING BORING BORING BORING
BORING BORING BORING BORING BORING BORING BORING
BORING BORING BORING BORING BORING BORING BORING
BORING BORING BORING BORING BORING BORING BORING
BORING BORING BORING BORING BORING BORING BORING
BORING BORING BORING BORING BORING BORING BORING
BORING BORING BORING BORING BORING BORING BORING
BORING BORING BORING BORING BORING BORING BORING
not boring

Sometimes boring is good. Being bored lets your brain freewheel and chug away in the background. Let yourself daydream, give yourself time to think. Forget about what you're trying to think about and let your subconscious grapple with the problem. Meanwhile, you can enjoy the weightless feeling of not having anything to think about. It's liberating!

I don't need much around me in order to work, I prefer simplicity and minimum distractions. When things are simple there is less to go wrong. I like to strip things down to their essentials in work and life. Think about things in a straightforward way. Try to be practical and decisive. Simplify your life to become more productive. Spend less energy managing chaos and have more time for reflection.

WANT BETTER NOT MORE

The thinking stage is the most
important aspect of any project.

The best ideas can be
remembered easily.

You need to know exactly what
you are trying to say before you
can communicate it properly.
By being brutal and cutting
out unnecessary elements, your
communication will be more effective.

DON'T WASTE TIME

Don't waste time.
Be productive.

DO NOT NO!

Don't stand in the way of your creative energy.

Allow yourself to create and make.
Don't block yourself or put barriers up.
It's easy to define what you do, to feel
secure within a narrow range.

Break out of the space you've made
for yourself.

Destroy the barriers! By making
exploration an important part of your
creative practice you are feeding the
creativity. And in the same way that you
give yourself permission to be creative,
pass on the enthusiasm to other people.

DON'T SAY NOTHING, SAY SOMETHING

It can be difficult to talk about your own work, especially when you're starting out, so it helps to find a way of speaking up that suits your style and that you feel comfortable with.

ASK MORE QUESTIONS
GET MORE ANSWERS!

How do you deal with work stress?
Manage your workload carefully – it's the
one thing I've learnt about staying happy.
Don't take on too much and don't spend
every waking hour worrying about projects.
Everything always works itself out and if
there is a crisis, a solution will be possible.

What if a project isn't going well?
Constant communication is the key to keeping
things running smoothly – if you are unsure
about something, ask. It's better to know what
people expect of you rather than make a guess.
Be clear about what you are due to deliver and
when, get it done and send it in time.

NO ANSWER IS THE WRONG ANSWER

An idea that at first feels wrong might prove to be just right. Don't rule anything out during your Initial thinking process. Don't hold yourself back – every solution can be valid. Let ideas develop before dismissing them, think freely and imaginatively.

YES & NO
NO & YES
YES & NO
NO & YES

YES & NO
NO & YES
YES & NO
NO & YES

MAKE YOUR MARK ON THE WORLD

Developing a personal
approach to work is
essential and something
that should happen to you
naturally as you grow
and develop.

Having a distinctive
approach is different
from working in one style.
Your personality and how
you view the world should
shine through your work.

If your work is an honest
reflection of who you are
as a person then it will
have longevity and
stay relevant.

A HOLIDAY FOR YOUR MIND

You can't work all the time, it's not good for you. Take extended breaks from work. Fill your brain with new experiences and information. Draw on these experiences when you get back to work. See things in a new way.

CHANGE YOUR LIFE

CHANGE

YOUR
LIFE

Every day.

THINK OF YOUR OWN

Be original in your thinking. Surprise yourself with your ideas.

Your primary influence should be you.

IDEAS

YOU
ARE
UNIQUE

Take your unique perspective on the world and communicate your own message.

YOU ARE UNIQUE

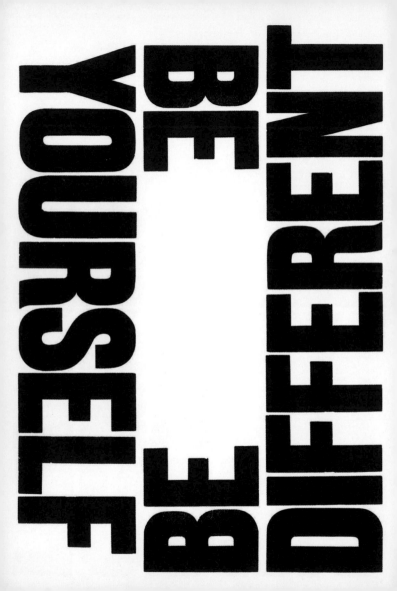

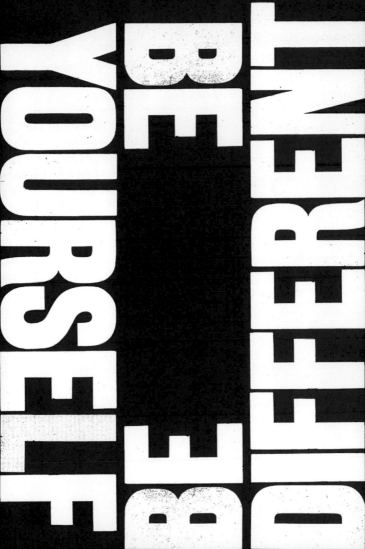

It's funny how something that initially could be seen as a weakness eventually helps you to define yourself and to stand out from the crowd.

You shouldn't feel that you have to be a certain type to succeed, the main thing is to be driven and believe in what you are doing.

ME

I AM

QUESTION YOURSELF

Don't get bored; push yourself and take on new challenges.

You have the answers, the answer is in the question.

NOTHING COMES FROM NOWHERE

Everything starts somewhere.

WHO ARE YOU WHAT DO YOU WANT?

Tell the world what you think – your opinion is as important as any other.

WHO ARE YOU WHAT DO YOU SAY?

FIND YOUR VOICE

**You already know
what you want to say.
You just need to find
out how to say it.**

WANT
TO BE
HEARD

I LIKE IT.

Curiosity is the key to everything.
Wanting to find out about the world
is a natural instinct. Feed your
curiosity by asking questions of
yourself and everybody around you.

WHAT IS IT?

USE YOUR FEAR

Sometimes the idea in my head doesn't work – maybe it's too complicated or over-stylised – that's when I start to strip things down and reduce an idea to its essence. Of course, you need to think about your audience and what you are trying to communicate, but that mustn't stop you from keeping ideas pure and individual.

Good work doesn't come out of compromise. We're all frightened, that's what drives everybody — insecurity about the future. My work is a way to try to deal with that. The work is positive but it comes from a place of insecurity, not angst exactly, but a feeling of wanting to prove myself.

Find out what it is
about your work that
doesn't make you
happy and change it.

MAKE YOUR WORK MAKE YOU HAPPY

AHEAD ONLY

Turn a weakness into a strength.

Don't accept that there's only
one way of doing something,
there are at least three.

Come at a problem from an
unexpected angle.

Don't feel that you need to
conform to be successful.

Try things that don't seem
obvious, they might surprise
you and lead you down a new path.

Sometimes it's hard to start.

It's easier not to start.

Starting can be difficult.

Go on, get going, make a start.
Once you've made that start it's hard to stop.
Now it's hard to stop!

STOP
START
STOP
START

WE LIVE AND LEARN

Be consistent with your message and don't worry too much about trying to fit in.

Deal with past successes and failures – think about how you can use them to build something new.

WE LEARN AND LIVE

Only by pushing yourself
can you move forward —
it's a trap to get too
comfortable. It's important
to use negative experiences
and challenges to find a
different way around things,
to create new opportunities
and ways of working.

GET IT WRONG GET IT RIGHT

A NEW IDEA EVERY DAY

Play to your strengths
and also try to work
on the areas you have
trouble with. Enthusiasm
goes a long way.

By putting positive messages and actions out into the world you are making life for everybody slightly better. When that positivity is reflected back it feels amazing. It makes you want to make a more positive contribution, whether that's through working with organisations that are effecting change, or simply in your day-to- day interactions with other people.

POSITIVE ENERGY MAKES POSITIVE WORK

MAKE TIME TO PLAY

MAKE TIME TO THINK

MAKE TIME TO REST

MAKE TIME TO WORK

JOIN

Seeing connections between things that don't initially seem to be related is a skill that can be developed.

THE

DOTS

By joining up ideas and people you can make amazing things happen.

Add in energy and enthusiasm to create momentum that is hard to stop.

FORGET EVERYTHING

It sounds exciting, doesn't it? Rejecting everything you've been taught. It's a necessary process. You should be able and willing to challenge your education. You choose who you believe.

What makes you happy?

A good balance of commercial
work and self-initiated
projects.

The sense of satisfaction
when a project has been
handed in and approved.

A good balance between
life and work.

Being in control of how
I spend my time and
having a creative outlet.

Ticking things off my
'to do' list.

Seeing a finished piece
of work that looks how
I hoped it would look.

Getting a positive reaction
to a piece of work.

GIVE THE JOY BACK

PROCESS
IS THINKING

MAKING
IS THINKING

QUESTIONING
IS THINKING

COMMUNICATING
IS THINKING

THE WORLD IS FOR YOU

People want to help
other people, it's a
human response.
Don't be afraid to ask for
help. You'll be surprised
how helpful people can
be, you just need to ask.

OPTIMISM IS NOT ALWAYS DUMB

I'm naturally optimistic, sometimes annoyingly so. I feel confident that things will work themselves out, even in the face of overwhelming evidence to the contrary. Keep your natural optimism, it's a valuable quality. Who knows, maybe everything will work out okay in the end.

PESSIMISM IS NOT ALWAYS DEEP

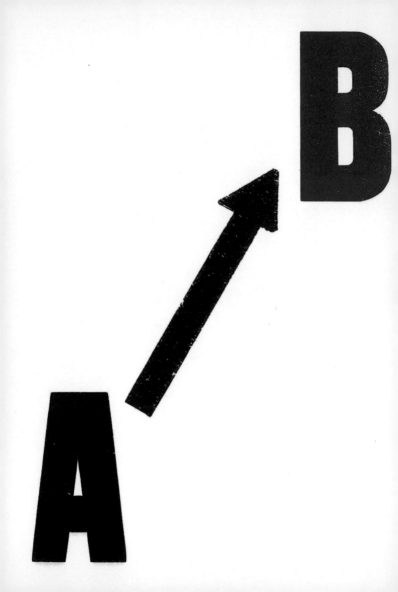

Thinking creatively is making a leap
between imagination and practicality.

MAKE WHAT YOU THINK

You need to know where you are going to feel motivated to get there.

THINK WHAT YOU MAKE

Be ambitious, push your work and yourself as far as you can.

WHO IS IT FOR?

Be your own worst critic. Be honest with yourself and about your work.

WHAT IS IT FOR?

Optimism, energy and enthusiasm make everything happen.

UNDERSTAND YOURSELF

Dig deep into yourself.
Question your motives and motivations.
Why do you do the things you do?
Why do you react in the way you do?
Do you make instant judgements?
Do you examine the evidence?
Do you respond with your head or your heart?

Think about everybody else.
Why do people do things the way they do?
Do people react in the way you intended?
Is your work connecting with people?
Do they ask questions about your work?
Are they interested in what you do?
Do people have to like your work?
Do you make it easy to understand your work?

UNDERSTAND EVERYONE

So, how was it? I hope you enjoyed reading this book and picked up some useful information. I said in the introduction, back at the beginning, that I don't have all the answers. I've found out what works for me through trial and error. You can only find out your own way of doing things by taking a chance and making that leap. You'll soon find out if you're on to something or if you need to change your approach. Success comes in lots of different ways. You'll know when you are achieving what you set out to achieve. You'll feel it inside and the pursuit of that feeling is what keeps us going. So go on, get on with it. Try it, see what happens and keep doing that until you get what you want!

Graphic artist Anthony Burrill combines a knack for simplicity that packs a punch, with analogue craft skills and powerful, positive messages. Burrill frequently collaborates with other forward-thinking creatives across disciplines spanning music, architecture, curation, education and more; pushing his traditional discipline of choice, letterpress printing, into bold new territories.

Words, gentle humour, no-nonsense communication and people are at the heart of Burrill's practice and his distinctive brand of upbeat messaging: its core DNA is one created through a long-standing passion for creativity, the power of simplicity and an innate curiosity about the world and people in it.

A.B.

```
Check
Spelling
Before
Printing!
```

It's a basic! This goes for everything, not just printing a poster or writing a book. Check every detail at least three times.

Never assume (see above).

Acknowledgements

With thanks to Emma Pidsley, Lucinda Humphrey and all at Ebury Publishing; special thanks to Elen Jones. Angharad Lewis, Erik Kessels, Ian Foster and Derek Stonham at Adams of Rye, Steve Fachiri and Tracey Day at Harvey Lloyd Screen Print, Greg Burne and Alastair Coe at Big Active, Raúl Goñi Fernandez, Vitor Manduchi, Karel De Mulder, Anthony Peters, Emily Gosling, Paul Plowman and Malcolm Goldie.

With love to Emma, Rosie and Jack Burrill.

POP PRESS

This paperback edition published in the United Kingdom by Pop Press, in 2020
First published as *Make It Now!* in the United Kingdom by Virgin Books, in 2017

1 3 5 7 9 10 8 6 4 2

Pop Press, an imprint of Ebury Publishing,
20 Vauxhall Bridge Road, London SW1V 2SA

Pop Press is part of the Penguin Random House group of companies whose
addresses can be found at global.penguinrandomhouse.com

Whilst every effort has been made to trace and acknowledge all copyright
holders, we apologise should there have been any errors or omissions in this
respect, and will be pleased to make the appropriate acknowledgements
in future editions

Anthony Burrill has asserted his right to be identified as the author of this Work
in accordance with the Copyright, Designs and Patents Act 1988

www.penguin.co.uk

A CIP catalogue record for this book is available from the British Library

ISBN 9780753558225

Design by Anthony Burrill and Emma Pidsley
Colour Origination by Altaimage Ltd, London
Printed and bound in China by C & C Offset Printing Co., Ltd

Penguin Random House is committed to a sustainable future for our business,
our readers and our planet. This book is made from Forest Stewardship
Council® certified paper.

MIX
Paper from
responsible sources
FSC
www.fsc.org   FSC® C018179